SPECKLED
&
SPOTTED

BREAKING FINANCIAL CEILINGS

SPECKLED & SPOTTED

BREAKING FINANCIAL CEILINGS

SINO AGUEZE

XULON PRESS

Xulon Press
2301 Lucien Way #415
Maitland, FL 32751
407.339.4217
www.xulonpress.com

Printed in the United States of America.

Paperback ISBN-13: 978-1-63129-042-8

Ebook ISBN-13: 978-1-63129-043-5

TABLE OF CONTENTS

INTRODUCTION

God's will for us is financial freedom. It's freedom from the credit consciousness that has kept so many bound, robbing us from living by divine design. It is freedom from the toiling of expending our mental, emotional and physical energy in exchange for little to nothing to show for it, while suffering from stress, pressure, pain, fatigue, loss and a list of sicknesses as a consequence. It is freedom from the idea that I'll have to work to earn a living by showing presence until death do me part. What if your bills were simply an afterthought? What if you lived with the "bird-consciousness" that Jesus talked about in Matthew chapter six, where they naturally had no consciousness of lack or want. What if you suddenly discovered that the easiest thing to make in life is money? And what if you could find yourself opened up to the idea that financial freedom frees you into fully living out your most authentic life — the life that God designed for you to live. It pulls you out from survival mode into thriving mode; helping you fulfill the covenant of Abraham: blessed to bless the families of the earth.

The lessons in this book was drawn from the business relationship between Jacob and his uncle, Laban. It took him twenty years to learn how to finally break free. But God had something much better than just freedom, He taught Jacob to master the financial system and to dominate it. He literally placed in his hands the master-key to controlling the market climates and conditions of his time. God wants to do the same thing for you. In this book, I've laid out eight principles that will help you break free from your financial struggles and challenges, and also help you thrive financially. These principles are pragmatic in nature, and attainable.

With God's help, you simply need to apply yourself, and commit yourself to the lessons drawn from this story. I am looking forward to celebrating your journey on the way to your freedom and financial success in life. Read on.

THE SALARY PRINCIPLE

CHAPTER 1

THE SALARY PRINCIPLE

Jacob was quite the trickster—deeply cunning. He had stolen his older twin brother's birthright, and the fatherly blessing that was rightfully due to Esau, the firstborn son. Running from the likely revenge of his brother's wrath, he was advised by his own mother, Rebekah, to go and live with his uncle Laban. Laban, who had two daughters, Leah and Rachel, was a well-seasoned devious trickster himself. Upon arriving at his uncle's house, he immediately developed strong feelings for Rachel, Laban's younger daughter. And only after a month of working for his uncle for free, tending to the care of the sheep and goats, was he asked what he would have as his salary. The question of offering to pay Jacob a salary came with a clear ulterior motive, howbeit, a sinister one at that. Apparently, within the space of thirty days, Laban knew that Jacob had a special ability of making businesses grow. It seemed that the covenant blessing of his grandfather, Abraham, which had been passed down to him from his father, Isaac, was evidently working. That covenant blessing gave him the ability to make magic happen. And that magic to make things happen was what Laban was after. He was going to use all the wits at his disposal to cap Jacob's financial ceiling at the salary level. For this reason, Laban offered him a salary as a means of obligating Jacob to work his farm —a modern day form of mental and financial slavery. He wanted Jacob exclusively committed to making him rich—to serve as a type of a cash cow if you will. As the story shows, he only saw Jacob as a tool to enriching himself.

> **Laban said, "You're family! My flesh and blood!" When Jacob had been with him for a month, Laban said, "Just because you're my nephew, you shouldn't work for me for nothing. Tell me what you want to be paid. What's a fair wage?"** **Genesis 29:14 MSG.**

It would appear at first that Laban was trying to do right by his nephew, Jacob, by offering him a salary in exchange for his services. However, being the devious trickster that he was, it was nothing more than a clever strategy to keep Jacob broke, beggarly and dependent. Jacob was clueless at this time of Laban's true intentions or perhaps naive about his uncle's true character. Maybe, he was blinded by the fact that Laban, his uncle, was family—his "blood" so to say. However, financial success has a way of turning families and friends into enemies. Money amplifies the true nature of a person. The money test is a test everyone in the kingdom must pass to walk into true wealth. Another test we must all pass is a deep desire to want to see others succeed and prosper. That is, we must be genuinely happy at the success of others. Money will always fly away from success critics. It will avoid haters like a plague.

In response to Laban's offer, Jacob agreed to work for seven years in exchange for Rachel's hand in marriage. The Bible shows that those seven years appeared as a few days because of the strong love that Jacob had for Rachel. This will bring us to principle number two: "the passion principal or the divine design principle," and we will fully discuss this in chapter two.

Early in life, it is extremely important that we find our calling. Life unfolds in the most beautiful way when it revolves around a central goal. And the earlier we discover this path, the better. Discovering the one thing we were born to do in life at the earliest time possible allows us to begin on time with investing the best part of our mental and physical energies toward it. We save time by avoiding to waste time. In a sense, we're giving the best of ourselves to the one thing that really counts, instead of spending half of our lives playing catch up because of the consequences of our bad choices. Knowing where you're headed in life helps to avoid the strenuous amount of guesswork that comes from navigating the future. Choosing the right path and being disciplined enough to stay on it is indeed a great plus. A question I often ask is: "if you knew then what you know now, how would you have lived any differently?" Am sure many of us would prefer to go back in time with the knowledge we now possess to maximize time and to live out our lives to its fullest capacity.

Jacob had set his mind on the prize on winning Rachel over, and his passion to win her over came with much focus and discipline. He would not deviate from it in-spite of the many obstacles and challenges that stood in his way. He made no excuses and avoided all distractions. In the same way, we should endeavor to give that kind of focus and discipline to our respective life goals. Jacob's deal with Laban was seven years of hard labor for the hand of Rachel in marriage. But all those seven years felt only like a few days.

Now Laban had two daughters; Leah was the older and Rachel the younger. Leah had nice eyes, but Rachel was stunningly beautiful. And it was Rachel that Jacob loved. So, Jacob

answered, "I will work for you seven years for your younger daughter Rachel." "It is far better," said Laban, "that I give her to you than marry her to some outsider. Yes. Stay here with me." So, Jacob worked seven years for Rachel. But it only seemed like a few days, he loved her so much   Genesis 29:16,19-20 MSG.

Laban had a clear strategy in place. The plan was to keep Jacob a working slave for as long as he could while all the time enriching himself. This plan was unknown to Jacob at the time. Jacob plunged head and feet into what he had to do to win Rachel as a price for his hard work. It would cost him seven years of hard labor. At the end of slaving for seven years, he looked forward with great anticipation and exhilarating joy to finally possess her as his bride and to fully make her his own. He'd been dreaming about this day for seven years with each passing day. No matter how strenuous the job got, Jacob endured it because of his love for Rachel.

On his wedding day however, Laban, the master-trickster, covered Leah with a robe and a veil so that Jacob would not recognize that she wasn't Rachel. I can only imagine how Laban convinced his first daughter, Leah, to go along with that devious plan. That conversation would go along the line of something that sounded like this: "hey Leah, you're the first daughter, and according to our tradition, you're to be married before Rachel. So, I am going to disguise you in a robe and a veil. Make sure that the room where you both would copulate on the wedding day is pitch black so that Jacob would never recognize you until the deed is done. Do this, and by this time tomorrow, you'd become a married woman, okay?" Leah, who in a sense was already in an unhealthy competition with her younger sister, would gently nod her head in agreement. She would have reasoned that the men found her younger sister as the more attractive one anyway; and so, to win at this game, she had to go along with her father's devious plan.

The plan appeared justifiable to both daddy and daughter. Leah went along because she saw this as an opportunity to finally have this one win over Rachel. So, that day came for Jacob. He was to finally marry the love of his life. He couldn't wait to reap the reward of his seven-year labor, or so he thought. But the trickster had a different plan in mind. It was a plan to beguile Jacob into working for him for another seven years.

> **Then Jacob said to Laban, "Give me my wife; I've completed what we agreed I'd do. I'm ready to consummate my marriage." Laban invited everyone around and threw a big feast. At evening, though, he got his daughter Leah and brought her to the marriage bed, and Jacob slept with her. (Laban gave his maid Zilpah to his daughter Leah as her maid.) Morning came: There was Leah in the marriage bed! Jacob confronted Laban, "What have you done to me? Didn't I work all this time for the hand of Rachel? Why did you cheat me?" "We don't do it that way in our country," said Laban. "We don't marry off the younger daughter before the older. Enjoy your week of honeymoon, and then we'll give you the other one also. But it will cost you another seven years of work."**
> **Genesis 29:21, 25-26 MSG.**

Laban was totally insincere. His motives were dubious at best. If he truly honored his father's tradition of marrying off the older one before the younger one, Jacob should've been informed of this from the start, and given the freedom to make that choice. However, this vital information was withheld from Jacob for the sole purpose of turning him into a cash cow for as long as He could. Remember, it had only taken the first thirty days of Jacob working for free for Laban, for Laban to see how profitable Jacob would become in growing Laban's LLC.

All along, Laban knew that because of Jacob, he had become an extremely wealthy man. This money machine of a person had to be kept oiled to keep the wheel of fortune running. It would take another seven years, totaling fourteen years to eventually payoff Rachel's bride price. This extension of time was what Laban had planned for from day one. And for such a cunning man as Laban, it wouldn't be a surprise that he had another devious plan in place for Jacob for the third seven years because we saw that at the end of the second seven years, he still offered him a salary to stay. So here goes Jacob again, toiling for another seven rigorous years. What was his first day back at work like as he stared away in the horizon over the vast acres of farmland, wondering about all the work he had to do for another seven years? He was forced to repeat this cycle simply for the sheer greed of one man. However, at the end of the fourteen years, notice how Jacob felt:

> **Soon after Rachel had given birth to Joseph, Jacob said to Laban, "Please release me so I can go home to my own country. Let me take my wives and children, for I have earned them by serving you, and let me be on my way. You certainly know how hard I have worked for you."**
> **Genesis 30:25-26 NLT.**

Jacob felt so unfulfilled. Although he had four wives and eleven boys over the course of fourteen years, he lacked the means to feed them or take adequate care of them. In fourteen years of toiling, he had no material or financial means to show for all that labor. Basically, he was broke and being broke ain't funny. Jacob understood that he couldn't subsist on his current salary. His salary would have kept him in a slave mode. The request that Jacob made to Laban to release him from toiling was a request for freedom. Financial freedom is God's will for everyone. It's built into our very DNA. Financial freedom frees us from the bondage of being self-absorbed. Living above our survival needs, allows us to think of others, and to find meaningful ways to pour our lives into others. Living free in this area of our lives should come with the same determination a slave would need to break out of any bondage. Whether it is bondage from addiction, abuse, fear or any inhibiting force; we should seek with the same determination to break free from financial bondage.

Multitudes, over the course of history have paid a huge price for freedom, and many among them died for it. The business of freedom demands serious effort. No lackadaisical approach would turn this monster around. Anything that's placing a ceiling on your happiness should be met with the same force as dealing with a cancerous plague that's determined to terminate your very existence. Many are used to living in bondage as an acceptable norm. In other words, they've normalized their bondage. They are unaware that they are in bondage or are completely oblivious to it. Settling and staying comfortable in any form of bondage is totally unacceptable. Show the heavens that you want out. Let your actions prove that you would not spend another minute in the house of bondage. Someone once said, "I'd rather die free, then live a day a slave." Am glad that at some point Jacob knew he couldn't continue life as a slave. He had to break free from it and break free he did.

America's Credit System is a form of bondage

My heart was broken when I first saw the credit system in America for what it really was. Multitudes are in bondage to it. Through the prevailing cultures and societal norms, a staggering majority of her population have been programmed by this system of slavery. It's a system of debt. The goal is debt servicing. The nation's financial system is built on borrowing. Its very financial culture is the culture of servicing debt. Students graduate with debt loans. Their lives into the real world begins with financial debt. And most of these student loans take forever to payoff. At this stage of life, many young couples borrow more money to acquire house mortgages with a thirty-year amortization. And for the first ten to fifteen years on that amortization, all their monthly payments go on paying on the interest only without a single dent on the principal. You'll still have to pay the property tax even after the house has been completely paid off. And depending on your own housing special circumstances, you may have to pay HOA fees, lease hold fees, city, state and federal taxes, and other fees you're not quite sure of even why you're paying them. Often, they'll borrow more money to acquire working vehicles for a five- or six-year loan term with additional interest fees, and then borrow more money by getting a few credit cards.

This system of living on borrowed money is why America as a nation is the most indebted nation in the world with a 20 trillion-dollar deficit. That debt continues to grow. The health of its entire financial system is founded and measured by one's credit score. They rather you have bad credit than no credit at all. Why shouldn't a nation want the financial wealth of its citizens to be measured by the acquisition and ownership of "zero-debt" assets, both fixed and liquid, instead of a credit score. And instead of a credit consciousness system, why not a debit consciousness system? Who convinced us that we need to live on borrowing? The rich folks do not live that way — the really rich ones own appreciating assets that keep on producing even while they're sleeping or playing golf. They work really hard to minimize all liabilities.

It's ironic that the two major things that make the world go around are not taught in any tertiary institution in the world — "finance and marriage." Why didn't they teach us or train us to develop multiple streams of income starting from elementary level? Why didn't they train us on how to live in a debit-consciousness system at the high school or secondary school level? Why wasn't that mentality built into us at a very early age? Who taught us anything about relationships? And yet, the world revolves around these two things. It seems to me that we got the wrong education after all. But the point is, God doesn't want us as slaves to any system.

Jacob desperately wanted out of financial bondage

Jacob knew it wasn't worth him continuing in the vicious cycle of financial bondage, and he desperately wanted out. Unknown to Laban, Jacob had already thought of a well-planned strategy on how to remedy his predicament. He knew that asking to be let go off his job would set the stage for it. It seemed that Jacob had a plan B. He didn't just ask to be let go without first putting into place a plan to breaking out of this mode. Why Laban kept insisting that he place Jacob on an ongoing salary that wouldn't help to give him the one thing he needed the most is mind boggling. He didn't really care about his nephew; no, not like Abraham did Lot. The story shows us that Laban wanted Jacob to remain at his mercy as a financial slave.

Have you ever met people who thought they owned your life? Maybe, people who derive so much pleasure at seeing you dependent on their mercy? They get a kick out of knowing you need them? It's rare to find people who are genuinely interested in helping you build a great life for yourself without any ulterior motive behind it. I wish we could introduce a different paradigm of the employer-employee relationship in the marketplace. I wish every employer would help each employee gain financial freedom. In other words, let the overall agenda be to lead each employee into financial freedom by initiating a workable plan for them to start their own businesses. The process may take some time, but it will be well worth it at the end. This will totally change the business culture of today. Sadly, the opposite is the predominant culture — the culture of wanting to keep you on the same salary level for decades with little to no raises in income — income that can rarely make a significant difference simply to keep the "money machine" running.

Unlike Jacob, it shouldn't take forever to find out that each of us must ultimately take personal responsibility for our own success. And don't allow anyone to tell you anything different. Your financial freedom is your responsibility. It is 100% up to you. Salaried positions have a subtle way of crippling you. It makes you unhealthily dependent. This is why for some; they tend to lose it when they lose a job. Being let go of a job can make one feel like the rug was pulled right from under them, leaving them completely hopeless. They start panicking and their hearts start palpitating because of the fear of possibly losing their homes and livelihood. Do you see how a job can become an idol, literally? The unhealthy attachment to a job is part of the reason why so many people are living contrary to their divine design. Many people will tell you as they grew older, they regretted not living out their true dreams and passions. They felt like they've wasted so many years living on the wrong pursuits of life. However, it is important to know that financial freedom is also a fact of life, and anyone willing can attain it if they choose to.

The Truth for Freedom Finally Dawns on Jacob

At some point, the truth about freedom began to dawn on Jacob too. He needed a clear plan from breaking this dependency on a salary. God showed him the way out. So, what was the plan B Jacob had cleverly planned with God's help and guidance? How was he going to finally turn things around? What exactly was his plan? We shall soon find out in chapter three. Just as God showed Jacob a way out, He is more than willing to show you a way out too. He wants you to break out of this unhealthy dependency on a salaried job. The salary principle applies to the majority. Many worked for years with nothing to show for it except for loss of vision, purpose, strength, enthusiasm for life, and all the other unaccountable lists of things difficult for us to quantify. Some have lost their health, and even died prematurely in the process.

Most of us all start out in life here. I wouldn't be exaggerating if I said more than 99.9% of us start here. Once we take on some sort of occupation, we start receiving paid salaries or wages. A salary is a monetary compensation for work done. It is man's evaluation of the value we bring to the table. There's nothing wrong with starting our financial journey in life this way. Jesus called it being faithful in the little. To make money, we will have to earn a salary at this phase of our lives. Think about the time when you first had a job at age sixteen. You earned hourly wages in exchange for work accomplished. This was essentially how you made some money. Very early in life, we make money by working on a job.

There are two ways money comes to us: through the rendering of a service or the delivery of a product. In any given market economy, these two ways of making money are the essential laws that drive demand and supply. Knowing how to grow from this beginner's phase to eventually mastering the market is the whole purpose of this book. In fact, God's will for our financial success is to literally control the market forces that shape market climate conditions. This was how Solomon became the wealthiest man on the entire planet. He controlled the market forces of his time and leveraged God's gift of wisdom to serve the nations of the earth. Because of his ability to solve deeply complex problems, the whole world looked to him for real solutions to real problems. The whole world became his clientele.

THE PASSION PRINCIPLE

CHAPTER 2

THE PASSION PRINCIPLE

This second principle is called the passion principle. Jacob had a strong passion to win Rachel over as his wife. For this reason, the seven years he spent working for Laban in exchange for the hand of Rachel felt like but a few days. May God grant us such a grace in this season. The passion principle has a far deeper meaning than the way the very word, "passion" is mostly understood by many in these times. A far better biblical rendering would be what I would call the "divine design" principle. Divine design has to do with the specific way God made you. He makes us all a certain way because of the specific assignment we all would have to accomplish with our lives. In other words, I am made the way I am because of what I was born to do. It is God's DNA strand woven to make up your own particular identity, and how your specific identity helps to define your destiny. Your identity serves your destiny. How you were made has everything to do with your life's purpose. It is divine because it originates from God. He alone created it, designed all of its intricacies and complexities, and breathed into it the success genes needed to bring it into fruition. In this divine design, the blueprint carries the backing of God's power to manifest it. No one knows us better than the one who made us. He knows every single thing about us even to the minutest details of our lives. Who we are and what we were meant to do with our lives are like two sides of the same coin, inseparably joined. And what God has joined together, let no man put asunder.

One irrefutable fact about choosing to live by divine design is that no other path, pursuit or purpose can rival it. There's simply no other life endeavor that can match it. The best decision after accepting Jesus as savior and Lord is following fully God's design for one's life. And to fully understand it, just take a closer look at how Jesus the Messiah lived. Almost three thousand years later, the whole world is still feeling the impact of His life. And all these amazing works because one man fully followed God's will for His life. May God keep us all, our eyes, on Him, until the day He calls us home.

In him was life; and the life was the light of men. John 1:4 KJV

His life was indeed the light of the world. His life illuminated the world. His life was the light of humanity. Without it, all humanity would completely be lost in the dark. He brought a new kind of life — the "God-kind." Through a glimpse of His life, we see into what life is all about, and how we ought to live it. He lived and displayed the God-Kind of life; not the man-kind. Only if we knew that the original life that we've been designed to live; the very one we were born into as new creations is the God-kind. The Scriptures affirm that all the children that you've given to me are for signs and for wonders — Isaiah 8:18. As gods in the earth, we ought to be a wonder to our generation. Every action we display ought to have the God-kind of strand woven through it. We should leave behind everything we do the mark of the finger-print of God. In these last days, there's never been a far more important time to look to Jesus, the author and finisher of our faith as our ultimate example for living.

Jacob's life showed that whenever he chose to follow that divine design, something extraordinary happened. We saw the beginning of it when he agreed to work for Laban his uncle for seven years in exchange for Rachel's hand in marriage. Everything he touched had God's success print on it. No wonder Laban wanted him caged up as a slave for life. But it is impossible to cage a man in alignment with his divine design. By the sheer law in the creative order, such a man will always come out on top. And such a man was Jacob out of whose lineage came forth the Messiah, Jesus.

And Jacob served seven years for Rachel; and they seemed unto him but a few days, for the love he had to her   Genesis 29:20 KJV.

Jacob served seven years for Rachel; but it only felt like a few days. Wouldn't it be amazing to accomplish a work of seven years in a few days? May God release His extraordinary wind to help us all accomplish such a feat in our time. And how can seven years of hard labor feel like a few days? Jacob worked in the heat of the day and in the frost of the night, and when you come to think of it, he worked for Rachel for a total number of fourteen years. The first seven years, he was beguiled by his uncle Laban, and was given Leah in marriage instead of the promised Rachel. So, he had to work another seven years for Rachel. And all these years of hard labor, coupled with all the injustices and mistreatments he had to endure — how could it all feel like a few days? How's that possible? That's precisely what divine design will accomplish for you. When you find yourself accomplishing things at the speed of spirit, that's a strong indication that one is living by divine design. Jesus puts it this way: "my meat is to do and to finish my father's will" — John 4:34. In other words, His very nourishment comes from accomplishing His Father's work on earth. They say it only took Jesus three and a half years to finish that work, but I think it took only twelve hours to do it. All of that three and half years led Him to the final twelve hours of His life where He finally accomplished the work He had come to do, and that was to give His life for the salvation of the whole world by dying the death of the cross. He fully lived out His divine design.

Living by Divine Design

All of God's creation is predicated upon a divine design. In surfing, one has to learn to flow with the waves in order to enjoy a successful surf. You'll have to cooperate with its divine design to achieve success at surfing. It's the same thing with electricity. Understanding how electricity works and cooperating with its laws is how we benefit from it. Learning to cooperate with divine order is key to a life of unending success. All true kingdom success is predicated upon seeking first the kingdom of God, and what God wants. God's divine design for life is found in Matthew chapter six and verses thirty and three.

> **Seek first God's kingdom and what God wants.**
> **Then all your other needs will be met as well**
> **Matthew 6:33 NCV.**

To truly enjoy all that God has planned for us, and all that God desires for us, we must live by the design of seeking first the kingdom of God. Our entire lives should be lived towards seeking God's kingdom earnestly. We should become kingdom seeking addicts. Yes, we should seek it like it was the only thing that mattered. I have already written a book on this called, "The Greatest Investment." I would like to encourage you to read it. It is a book that was written to reveal the heart of our "M633 Movement." It helps to shed light on what we're all about as a ministry.

So, what does it truly mean to seek first the kingdom of God? It simply means to live all of your life through the lens of a soul winner. It is when all about you becomes all about winning lost souls to Jesus. Winning the lost becomes the highlight of your life, rather than living to service debt. All you see is souls; all you hear is souls and all you live for is souls. It's when all of your life's decisions and choices are shaped by seeking and saving the lost. I discovered that all the angels of God rejoice over a single soul that turns to God in repentance. There's no other record in Scripture where God's angels rejoice over any other thing in all of creation. They don't rejoice when we get promoted on the job or when we buy a new house or when we graduate from college. These things maybe important to us down here, but they're not significant up there. God's greatest treasure on earth are people. And the angels know this to be true. And why do you think they make such an ado about souls? Because it is heaven's most important cause. And he that wins souls is wise — Proverbs 11:30. The highest form of wisdom in the kingdom is aligning our entire lives with winning souls. It is making your life revolve around this one central goal. This poem, which you'll find in the book I wrote called "Greatest Investment," explains it all. It is called, "What if."

What if:

What if our thoughts were soul winning thoughts?

What if our decisions were soul winning decisions?

What if our actions were soul winning actions?

What if our money was soul winning money?

What if our assets were soul winning assets?

What if every day was a soul winning day?

What if our time was primarily a soul winning time?

What if our jobs were seen as soul winning jobs?

What if our dreams were soul winning dreams?

What if our prayers were soul winning prayers?

What if every platform was a soul winning platform?

What if our very lifestyle was a soul winning lifestyle?

What if all roads in life lead to the saving of a soul?

We're yet to realize the full power of living our lives this way. In fact, our very growth in Christ is directly tied to this divine design. There's something about winning souls that takes your personal growth in Christ to the next level. It literally touches everything else. Unfortunately, we've reduced Christian growth to classroom lectures, rather than a real-life experience — an experience that only comes while we're on the job in the mission field winning people to Jesus.

The power of the gospel and the manifestation of that power is tied to this design. Miracles, signs and wonders answer to this design. Everyone is asking why we don't see the miracles of the Bible in our times as often and as frequent as we should. Mark chapter sixteen and verses twenty tells us that the Lord was working with them with signs following as they went forth to preach the gospel. Less preaching; less power — Romans 1:16. But it is the preaching of the gospel of Jesus Christ to the lost world where the real power flows — Acts 8:5-8. Some are preaching it to the saved, but the saved better take it to the lost if they ever want to see real miracles, signs and wonders.

The true value of our time on earth is tied to this design. Because time is limited, it creates a sense of urgency. As a result, we can choose to give it all we've got by focusing on what's important.

We fully live when we live this way fully. Imagine a life totally lived out for God's glory — yes, a life completely dedicated to reaching the lost. This is the most important paradigm shift needed among God's people in this generation.

For whosoever will save his life shall lose it; but whosoever shall lose his life for my sake and the gospel's, the same shall save it. For what shall it profit a man, if he shall gain the whole world, and lose his own soul? Or what shall a man give in exchange for his soul? Whosoever therefore shall be ashamed of me and of my words in this adulterous and sinful generation; of him also shall the Son of man be ashamed, when he cometh in the glory of his Father with the holy angels Mark 8:35-38 KJV.

We've often quoted these Scriptures in a fragmented way but read it again within its full context and something beautiful emerges. Jesus said we are to give our lives for Him, and for the sake of the gospel. He places His own life on the same plane with the gospel's as if they are eternally joined. A man's soul can live in want of gaining the whole world and still be lost at the end of it all. A lost soul is not only a soul separated from God, but also a soul in chase of the emptiness of this life. It's a soul wasted on the vanities of this life. In other words, a soul that's not invested in the gospel is defined by Jesus as a lost soul. What can a man give in exchange for his soul? What can he spend it on? Every living soul should live for Christ and live for the sake of His gospel. You'll notice how Jesus concludes that text with telling us that if we become ashamed of Him and His words (the gospel), He also would become ashamed of us when He appears in the glory of His father and His holy angels.

This divine order of God's kingdom is first generic in nature. In other words, it is for everyone who has come to faith in Christ Jesus. God is calling each of us to align completely and wholeheartedly with this order of His kingdom. Seeking first the kingdom of God and His righteousness is in itself the law of the divine design. It is only when we are fully aligned with this divine order that we can now walk into our own particular divine design, that is, the design for our respective lives and callings. Divine design is how your unique self expresses the central purpose of your life. It is the forging and merging of man's inner self with his cause. God, the designer, designed us in such a way that enables us to fulfill a specific purpose for our lives. A simple way to say this is God made you a certain way because of what He intends to accomplish through your life. Your identity expresses your destiny. The making of you, your design, has to address the specific thing you were born to do.

Jacob labored for seven years but it felt like a few days. He had a central vision at the time — he simply wanted Rachel's hand in marriage. Somehow, the joy of winning Rachel over was so strong that time felt condensed. His love for her was so compelling, not one single obstacle stood in his path because of it. Mountains felt like molehills and difficult challenges felt like opportunities. Ultimately, Jacob's love for Rachel made him work for a second seven years for her. Imagine what such a passion like that would do for you. Imagine such a flame on the altar of your heart igniting you to accomplish great feats for the kingdom of God. This is exactly how divine design works. It is a lifestyle graced with God's precious oil. It is sailing with heaven's wind behind your ship. Your divine design expresses your most authentic self — yes, it expresses your unique fingerprint. Our lives must revolve around a central goal by making your unique self (temperament, gifts and graces) align with your particular calling. The more you bridge the gap between the two the more explosive you'll become.

One of the primary ways of discovering and developing your divine design is to pay attention to how God uses you. It's important that you work to understand how your gifts flow. Each gift has a uniqueness, a rhythm, a secret code, a rarity about it. For instance, not everyone sings the same way or solves complex problems the same way. And just as your particular fingerprint is unique, your gift is tied to a design plan particular only to you. That distinct signature is what sets apart your particular gift from all the others even within the same genre. It's the signature mark of your gift. And to understand the workings of your gift, you must listen, observe and pay attention to the things that make your gift magical.

(1 Timothy 4:14 GW)

"Don't neglect the gift which you received ..."

Ask yourself, "What kind of beautiful things have to come together to enable this gift to operate at full capacity? What makes it both powerful and explosive? What makes it tick?" Pay attention to the details that define your gifts. For instance, my main mission is to help people experience the manifest and transformative presence of God. This gift of grace is activated through intense fasting, prayer and spending much quality time in the presence of God. Then it's released through in-depth revelation of the teaching of God's Word and worship. Does that make sense? These activities empower God's gifts to me. In order for your gifts to function at full capacity, you too, will be required to risk stepping out of your comfort zone.

THE PARTNERSHIP PRINCIPLE

CHAPTER 3

THE PARTNERSHIP PRINCIPLE

J acob had been offered a salary three different times. It was known from Jacob's statement that the reason for this continuous offer was to keep him imprisoned as a financial slave. Laban only thought of himself, and really didn't care about Jacob's future. Like most corporate companies today, employing people with the goal of helping them live financially free is hardly the objective. Most don't even care about the well-being of their employees. If every employer hired people with the objective of empowering them to become entrepreneurs and financially free, it would revolutionize the business world overnight.

> "In the twenty years I've worked for you, ewes and she-goats never miscarried. I never feasted on the rams from your flock. I never brought you a torn carcass killed by wild animals but that I paid for it out of my own pocket—actually, you made me pay whether it was my fault or not. I was out in all kinds of weather, from torrid heat to freezing cold, putting in many a sleepless night. For twenty years I've done this: I slaved away fourteen years for your two daughters and another six years for your flock and you changed my wages ten times. If the God of my father, the God of Abraham and the Fear of Isaac, had not stuck with me, you would have sent me off penniless.

But God saw the fix I was in and how hard I had worked and last night rendered his verdict."
Genesis 31:38 MSG.

So, you'll notice that Jacob fully understood Laban's intentions for wanting to keep him on a salary level in-spite of the tremendous value he was bringing to the table. Jacob was solely responsible for all of Laban's wealth; and yet, he was barely making ends meet. At some point, like everyone else, he had to ask Laban for the freedom to take complete charge of his own life as the provider and breadwinner for his family. Every real man has this innate desire to want to provide for his family. And this desire is inborn in them as part of their divine design. If only so many others knew the real intentions of companies and corporations who have no real interest in the prosperity of their employees. I have seen so many mega churches operate the same way. They use people as cash cows. How many churches put people under a salary while mortgaging their musical talents and robbing them of their creative properties all in the name of building the church? Why we don't want people to truly prosper baffles me. The truth is to prosper in this life, we must wholeheartedly seek the prosperity of others.

Jacob had worked for Laban's two daughters for fourteen years, and still had nothing to show for it — nothing in financial or material terms. He knew nothing was going to significantly change unless he broke out of this salary level. He had given his situation some thought and figured that he had to transition from being paid a salary to entering into an equity partnership with Laban. He was tired of getting the crumbs from his own fully baked cake. Partnership in the business would begin the journey to his financial freedom. He didn't just want to make a salary, he wanted to build wealth. And yes, there's a huge difference between the two. Obviously, making money and building wealth are not the same thing.

Our Deep-Seated Beliefs can Sabotage our Financial Success

A self-sabotaging trait I often see among believers is rooted in the idea that excess wealth is somehow wrong or evil. However, the Scriptures tell us that a good man leaves an inheritance for his children's children — Proverbs 13:22; and that the profit of the earth is for all — Eccl. 5:9. That means God expects you to build up enough wealth that would last two generations. And that's just a part of being a good man. How much more a righteous man or woman? We not only build wealth for our immediate family, but we build to bless the world. We build wealth to advance the cause of Jesus Christ. This motive drives the need to create and build wealth, including excess wealth. No one ever achieves anything of significance without becoming serious about their own particular pursuit. Many Christians haven't really decided that building wealth is an important part of their calling. In other words, making money is not that important at all. They fail to see that it is God who gives us the power to create wealth because creating wealth as a means of fulfilling the Abrahamic covenant is important to God — Deuteronomy 8:18. God wants us blessed so that we can bless the world. Money not only has a role to play on this planet; it is also indispensable to advancing the cause of Christ. Every revival or move of God in history generates enormous wealth–the wealth to place the love of God on display. The glory of the latter house is directly tied to silver and gold–Haggai 2:8-9. Jacob's wealth was called his glory

— Genesis 31:1. Money is important for the things that have to do with money. It answers all things — Ecclesiastes 10:19. It solves problems in the natural realm. It is one of the most dangerous weapons in the hands of the righteous against the kingdom of darkness. Imagine how many lives we can change with the means and power to do it. Let the understanding of what one can do with money make you become serious about building financial wealth. We've tiptoed and cringed around this subject for far too long. We don't even know what to believe anymore. Others have self-defeating beliefs based upon false assumptions driving their decisions and actions. Jesus taught us to do business in the marketplace. In both parables, He wants us to develop a 100% profit mentality on all the investments that we make as a starter.

> **Soon after Rachel had given birth to Joseph, Jacob said to Laban, "Please release me so I can go home to my own country. Let me take my wives and children, for I have earned them by serving you, and let me be on my way. You certainly know how hard I have worked for you."**
> **Genesis 30:25-26 NLT**

Jacob tells Laban, his uncle, to release him from servitude. In other words, Jacob requested to be set free from financial bondage. You only need a release if you're bound. Financial servitude is just another modified form of slavery, and Jacob wanted out. Unfortunately, it took him fourteen years to finally grasp it. It's so sad that many of God's people are not even aware that they are in financial bondage. They've normalized it. They were literally born into a financial system that's bent on making financial slaves out of people. As a result, they settled and never questioned the status-quo or the system. Jacob wanted to feel like he owned something. He wanted to own his own assets — something he could proudly pass on to his children after his death. May God release you from all forms of bondage, including financial bondage. You live to serve the King not to service debt.

> **"Please listen to me," Laban replied. "I have become wealthy, for the Lord has blessed me because of you. Tell me how much I owe you. Whatever it is, I'll pay it."**
> **Genesis 30:27-28 NLT**

Knowing fully well of Jacob's value to his corporation, all he could think of was keeping him at the salary level. He was simply willing to give him a raise but that was all he was ever going to do about it. He was only thinking about himself. He neither listened nor understood Jacob's concerns. Jacob had become the sole reason for Laban's wealth. Why wouldn't Laban want for Jacob to enjoy a piece of the pie? Why wouldn't he bring him on as a partner? And why wouldn't he want for Jacob what he wanted for himself? Laban's insatiable greed had a stronghold on him. He had no desire to want to see his own nephew prosper, and that's deeply unfortunate.

> **Jacob replied, "You know how hard I've worked for you, and how your flocks and herds have grown under my care. You had little indeed before I came, but your wealth has increased enormously. The Lord has blessed you through everything I've done. But now, what about me? When can I start providing for my own family?"**
> **Genesis 30:29-30 NLT**

Every real man wants to provide for own his family. He wanted an empowering partnership deal considering the value he was bringing to the table. He knew that neither a salary nor a salary raise would cut it. Despite all of Jacob's effort to explain his situation, Laban was so self-absorbed. As a consequence, Laban did what he does best. He asked him how much of a raise he would want. Laban didn't really have much of anything until Jacob showed up in his life as a gift from God. He had failed to truly see his nephew as a blessing from God. His familiarity with Jacob's natural heritage had blinded him from seeing that his nephew was the sole custodian of the Abrahamic covenant. He had become completely oblivious that Jacob had on himself the magic to make things happen. God's supernatural grace on him made the "rag to riches" phenomenon a reality. Laban, like most bosses, had the mistaken idea that as long as they were paying the salary, then their employees didn't deserve anything else. You'll often hear them say you're simply doing what you were paid to do. It is wrong to treat high value employees this way. For Jacob, he wasn't just a high valued employee, he was solely responsible for the growth and expansion of Laban's corporation. Jacob had singlehandedly transformed a small sole proprietorship into a 500-fortune company. God's grace on his life made it all possible.

"What wages do you want?" Laban asked again   **Genesis 30:31 NLT.**

For some strange diabolical reason, Laban couldn't let go of trying to force on Jacob the need to stay on a salary. Apparently, he had become clueless to what Jacob wanted changed in their business relationship. Jacob wanted a pathway toward financial freedom. What man or woman on this planet wouldn't want to feel like they can stand on their own two feet? Who wants to remain at the mercy of feeding on crumbs or living at the mercy of another man? Even within the animal kingdom, the child at some point must weave off their parent's dependence. God stood back from Adam to see what he would call the animals. He was teaching the first man how to stand on his own feet. Ultimately too, this is what every parent would want for their child. Dependence on God is not a healthy excuse from taking personal responsibility for one's life. However, Jacob knew better this time around, although, it took him fourteen years of slaving to finally realize it.

> **Jacob replied, "Don't give me anything. Just do this one thing, and I'll continue to tend and watch over your flocks"**
> **Genesis 30:31 NLT.**

At last, Jacob had figured out a way to break free from his uncle's control. So much thought and planning had gone into it. He had a clear strategy on how he was going to turn the situation around. This painful process of planning would infer that he had given his situation a lot of thought and had concluded that he couldn't continue to live like a slave. He simply couldn't fathom how he was going to live perpetually in debt, and possibly, drag his entire family into it. His desperation for change brought God to his aid. God heard his cry and remembered His covenant with Abraham, Jacob's grandfather.

You're going to have to get sick and tired about getting sick and tired of your situation for things to change. There has to be some desperation for change. Those who become satisfied with the status-quo hardly ever see the need for

35

change. They've become immune to change because they're accustomed to a conditioning of containment. Some are deeply terrified that breaking out of a box might reveal the weaknesses they're unwilling to face up to because they'll finally have to admit that they're too lazy to do the work required for change. So, they'll rather continue with the false belief that nothing good happens for them as a means of avoiding the cost for change, and as a cover-up mechanism for coping with failure. The Bible teaches that the destruction of the poor is their poverty. Many, however, finally embrace change only after they've hit rock bottom.

It was Jacob's time to set his uncle up for an interesting chess game. It was a game he was both planning on playing and winning. God had mapped out for him all the moves he'll need to make to win in life. Above all, God wanted His covenant child free, so that, through Jacob, and Jacob's twelve sons, out of which the twelve tribes of Israel were born, the entire lineage of the seed of Abraham would live free. Freedom is at the very heart of the gospel — at the very heart of God Himself. His first commandment is a command for us to never bow down to any idols. He would have us never to be in bondage to anyone or anything. We cannot serve mammon; we must only serve God.

> **Jacob replied, "Don't give me anything. Just do this one thing, and I'll continue to tend and watch over your flocks"**
> **Genesis 30:31 NLT.**

Jacob negotiated for something far better than a salary. He wanted partnership. He wanted some equity in a business he had helped grow into a major corporation. Even though he had requested for a small amount of equity, it was at least a step higher than a salary. Owning something or being a part owner in a business venture not only gives one a far better incentive to work, but also reveals a part of God's wisdom in creating and building wealth. God is calling us to ownership. He is calling us to live a life of acquiring assets while minimizing liabilities. He is showing us how to make money work for us even while we sleep at night. He is telling us to set in motion a money-making machine that would continually produce wealth even while we're engaged in the other activities of life. Jacob, for the first fourteen years had owned practically nothing. He had nothing to his name, and nothing to build with or build from. He was a slave trapped with the crumbs falling from the master's table. He was earning some insufficient income, barely able to meet his necessities, but was not building any measure of wealth. Making money and building wealth are two different things as previously stated.

In the world's economy, you're going to have to negotiate for what you're worth. Very often, in a job-setting, a change in your financial status is not just going happen without your willful action. Most bosses will never suggest it. It will be up to you to negotiate that next level promotion. However, you're going to have to earn that negotiation. You earn it by the value you bring to the table. For Jacob, negotiating for this partnership was a means to a greater plan that God had already revealed to him. It would become the doorway into his financial freedom. God wants you financially free. Financial freedom empowers you to take command of the dawn. It helps you have a better handle on life.

Jacob Lays Out His Proposal

So, how did Jacob lay out this proposal before Laban? His plan contained secrets — secrets that would lead to his financial freedom. His plan was built on a divine strategy; howbeit, a winning one. Laban had no idea that Jacob's proposal was going to turn the table. If he had known it, he wouldn't have hastily agreed to it.

> **"What wages do you want?" Laban asked again. Jacob replied, "Don't give me anything. Just do this one thing, and I'll continue to tend and watch over your flocks. Let me inspect your flocks today and remove all the sheep and goats that are speckled or spotted, along with all the black sheep. Give these to me as my wages. In the future, when you check on the animals you have given me as my wages, you'll see that I have been honest. If you find in my flock any goats without speckles or spots, or any sheep that are not black, you will know that I have stolen them from you." "All right," Laban replied. "It will be as you say."**
> **Genesis 30:31-34 NLT.**

Jacob asked for the speckled and spotted sheep and goats, along with all the black sheep as his wages. And Laban agreed. Laban agreed because it was very rare to produce speckled and spotted sheep and goats, and to find full colored black sheep was almost unheard of. Laban must have thought to himself that Jacob had finally entrapped himself into a third phase of perpetual financial bondage. From a natural stance, Laban couldn't see Jacob's vantage point. Maybe, he might have considered Jacob a fool who had finally dug his own pit from which there was no coming out. Unraveling this plan through the chapters of this book would prove quite an adventure for the seeker who genuinely desires not only to be financially free, but also to build a legacy of wealth for God's glory. Jacob had planned to live honestly. He would not steal, cheat or tarnish his integrity. His business model was built on honoring God. Out there, in the field, where no human eye was watching, Jacob was always going to do right by God. And because he honored God, God in-turn, honored him.

THE VALUE PRINCIPLE

CHAPTER 4

THE VALUE PRINCIPLE

Jacob was a man of worth. He had an "added-value" mentality. He brought value to the table. Every child of God should always think in terms of adding value. From the first day Jacob helped out his uncle Laban, it only took him thirty days to see that Jacob had that x-factor in building successful businesses. Jacob had tremendously increased Laban's profits by such a margin, and from then on, Laban was going to hold on to his nephew as long as he could. When Jacob asked for Laban's daughter, Rachel, in marriage, the bride price was to be seven years of work. And in that time, we noticed Laban's testimony of Jacob's business expertise.

> **"Please listen to me," Laban replied. "I have become wealthy, for the Lord has blessed me because of you. Tell me how much I owe you. Whatever it is, I'll pay it."**
> **Genesis 30:27-28 NLT**

Laban said he had become wealthy because of God's extraordinary favor upon Jacob's life. Jacob thought of things in terms of adding value. Truth is, poor people think in terms of maintenance, but rich people think it terms of an "added-value" leadership mentality. For instance, the poor are simply concerned with limiting their contributions within the boundaries of their job description working forty hours a week. They simply do what they're told with a maintenance mode mentality and can barely wait to get off of the clock. They think in terms of time — their nine-to-five Jobs. However, the rich think in terms of a holistic approach to the overall strategic vision of the company. They're constantly looking for ways to move it forward whether it's their job description or not. They bring up growth and expansion ideas by looking for ways to increase the company's effectiveness, efficiency, productivity and profits. Simply stated, they look for meaningful ways to add real value. Like Jacob, the goal is taking a small business and turning it into a mega corporation. The rich and prosperous engage in self-study and research learning things about what the competition does best, while seeking to incorporate the best practices. They're outside the box thinkers and are always working hard to be at the cutting edge of innovation.

Christians should have a global trademark of bringing serious value to the marketplace and to the world at large. We should be known for this, letting our light shine — Matthew 5:16. People all over the world should want to fill all job vacancies with Christians because of the value they bring to the table. People should be able to say about us what Laban said about Jacob — that we are earth movers and shakers. That we've mastered the science on how to grow a seed into a forest. There have been many others in the Bible who have had similar testimonies.

> **The Lord was with Joseph, so he succeeded in everything he did as he served in the home of his Egyptian master. Potiphar noticed this and realized that the Lord was with Joseph, giving him success in everything he did. This pleased Potiphar, so he soon made Joseph his personal attendant. He put him in charge of his entire**

household and everything he owned. From the day Joseph was put in charge of his master's household and property, the Lord began to bless Potiphar's household for Joseph's sake. All his household affairs ran smoothly, and his crops and livestock flourished. So, Potiphar gave Joseph complete administrative responsibility over everything he owned. With Joseph there, he didn't worry about a thing—except what kind of food to eat! Joseph was a very handsome and well-built young man
Genesis 39:2-6 NLT.

Joseph, like Jacob, completely revolutionized Potiphar's company. Potiphar saw that everything Joseph touched prospered. Joseph's entire approach to business was greatly admired by his master, and as a result, he made him the CEO of his company. How was Joseph able to reveal God in the business arena? Or better yet, how did Potiphar, director of Pharaoh's secret service, see the Lord at work in Joseph's life? Joseph's ability to turn that much profit in a short time astounded Potiphar. It seemed that everything he touched turned to gold. He had grown his company to great heights in Egypt. You see, the Lord wants to reveal more of Himself to the world in the marketplace. The language of the gospel in the marketplace is called the gospel of results. In the business world, God still owns the silver and the gold, but He made it all for the church to possess it, and to use it to display His love to a dying world in a tangible form.

However, to succeed in this life, you must bring real value to the table. You must think and act in terms of value — producing indelible and undeniable results on the stage of life. It truly pays to serve God and this book is designed to show you how. He wants to put his favor on your life on display for the world to see. And when you're gone, the world should greatly miss your absence and deeply feel the loss. If you're serious about learning how to be a man or woman of value, read my book on "Building Capacity." Jacob over the course of 20 years, had become a man of tremendous capacity for building corporations. He had been mentored by the best teacher — the Holy Spirit.

> **"What wages do you want?" Laban asked again. Jacob replied, "Don't give me anything. Just do this one thing, and I'll continue to tend and watch over your flocks. Let me inspect your flocks today and remove all the sheep and goats that are speckled or spotted, along with all the black sheep. Give these to me as my wages. In the future, when you check on the animals you have given me as my wages, you'll see that I have been honest. If you find in my flock any goats without speckles or spots, or any sheep that are not black, you will know that I have stolen them from you."**
> **Genesis 30:31-33 NLT.**

Jacob was setting Laban up. When he asked for a partnership resulting into an equity share of the company, he already had a God given plan on how he was going to finally turn the tide. The real story of his rag to riches starts here. Apparently, God had given Jacob a success blueprint on how to win in the business world. God's plan was failure proof. By asking for the speckled and spotted animals, his original plan centered on simply breeding them in the natural order. Jacob was thinking on a natural plane, like any other farmer. He was thinking really small, hoping that the few speckled and spotted sheep would mate and produce a smaller flock enough to make a living on. Many Christians have settled on just getting by. In their heads, they feel like they deserve more; but, in their hearts, they don't really believe that they should or can have more. We sub-consciously abort God's plan for abundance for our lives through a false humility. You'll often hear people say things like, "I simply want just enough to take care of my family." Somehow, they forget, that in God's economy, there are no shortages. To the contrary, God's wealth is inexhaustible. The creation order speaks of abundance and extravagance. Why would a man ejaculate billions of spermatozoon seeds when all you need is one sperm to produce a child? Why would God place billions and trillions of planets simply to decorate the skies with stars? The oceans are filled with innumerable species of fish as the sky is with birds. God doesn't just make a green grape, but also a black and red one too. Everything about God is a show of abundance and pure extravagance. In our small mindedness and shortage mentality, we often think that things are running out. Open your mind and heart to abundance. There's a world out there who would need all the help they can get, and your "barely enough" won't do it.

Making Money Vs Building Wealth

There's a clear difference between making money, even lots of it, from building sustainable wealth. The goal is to build generational wealth. The Bible teaches us that a good man leaves an inheritance for his children's children — Pr. 13:22. This implies that we should endeavor to build a form of wealth to last at least two generations. I am of the personal belief that God is moving His own children to transition from working a job to owning multiple streams of income. In God's creative order, we see the pattern of a divine system at work in the seed. God places within the seed the power to produce at will. From a single seed, we can produce a forest of crops. The cycle is predicated upon the law of seedtime and harvest. God doesn't need to command vegetation out of the ground every quarter of the year. It is simply something He had to do one time. The seed self-sustains and self-produces. Similarly, God is asking us to apply the same principle to wealth-building. That is, to set a machine in place that continues to produce on-going wealth day and night even while we're sleeping. Setting this money-making machine in place is the wisdom for the hour for us as people of God. This way, you're not at the mercy of people and events or times and seasons. This is the way we ought to be thinking about building wealth. At some point, it becomes a well-oiled machine effortlessly producing income for you, while releasing you from the burden of working yourself to the bone trying to keep up with paying your bills.

In Abraham Maslow's theory on the law of the hierarchy of human needs, he puts forth a hypothesis that people function at their highest capacity and competence when they transcend their survival needs. Living in survival mode stands at odds with God's will for us. God's will for us all is to have our bills paid as an after-thought. In other words, our day to day bills shouldn't even factor into our thought processes. It should never become a part of the equation or factor into our consciousness. God's kingdom should be the one thing driving our daily existence. Birds, according Jesus, have no consciousness of lack — not one. Their minds are fixed on the consciousness of having their daily bread met without any thought, effort or doubt. It's a consciousness that's a part of their DNA. And are we not far more valuable than birds? May God deliver us from this fallen order. May we all heed the Spirit's call to fully embrace God's will for us on living the abundant life.

It's important that we keep at working on ourselves. We need to leverage every opportunity to work on improving our capacities — all seven of them. Our spiritual, mental, emotional, vocational, financial, physical and life's purpose capacities need constant work. The last level of your growth is the level where your life has been capped. In other words, to go up, you'll have to work up. Settling or staying stagnant in life is unacceptable because anything that's not growing is dying. Self-improvement is not a gift of grace; it is a personal responsibility we'll have to take to better our lives. As long as you're moving forward, you're bound to breaking the ceilings over your life, while making tremendous progress all at the same time.

In the African continent I grew up in, we barely had any major industries at the time. They were all benched marked overseas. Africa produced the largest percentage of diamonds in the world, but the industry was benched-marked in the United Kingdom. Sudan produced tea, and Kenya, coffee. Nigeria produced crude oil but processed it abroad. We sell our goods as raw products for little to nothing, and then buy them back for ten times the price. We lost 70% of added value in all of our products because we had no processing skills or plants. Other nations got rich over our inability to think in terms of value.

> **There wasn't a blacksmith to be found anywhere in Israel. The Philistines made sure of that "Lest those Hebrews start making swords and spears." That meant that the Israelites had to go down among the Philistines to keep their farm tools— plowshares and mattocks, axes and sickles—sharp**

and in good repair. They charged a silver coin for the plowshares and mattocks, and half that for the rest. So when the battle of Micmash was joined, there wasn't a sword or spear to be found anywhere in Israel—except for Saul and his son Jonathan; they were both well-armed
1 Samuel 13:19–MSG

I used to ask often, "where are the blacksmiths of Africa?" Why is the African continent the richest continent in terms of manpower, minerals and other indispensable resources, and yet, her people are among the most impoverished people groups in the world. Africa is more of a consumer-oriented continent than it is a producer, and as a consequence, loses about 70% of added value on her priceless resources. I believe all of this result from Africa's lack of blacksmiths.

Blacksmiths are those who understand the science of things: the science of developing a nation from a third world class to a first world class. This elite group of people control processes— which is the means of processing raw materials to create an added value for their products. Blacksmiths are a highly valued skilled work force. They leverage their nation's resources to help compete in the global markets of the world for the prosperity and posterity of its people.

I have also found myself asking lately, "where are black-smiths in the kingdom of God?" Israel as a nation had no blacksmiths during the reign of King Saul. They lacked the knowledge on how to produce fighting, farming and feeding tools necessary for the survival of a people. They had to travel to the land of the Philistines to make tools and sharpen their axes and plowshares and paid a silver coin for it — a much more costly price. During the time of war, there was not found in all Israel a single sword to fight with. And the

Philistines made sure that there were no blacksmiths with the skill needed to produce swords and plowshares. All the manufacturing and processing plants were benched marked in the land of the Philistines.

> **And he carried away all Jerusalem, and all the princes, and all the mighty men of valour, even ten thousand captives, and all the craftsmen and smiths: none remained, save the poorest sort of the people of the land. And all the men of might, even seven thousand, and craftsmen and smiths a thousand, all that were strong and apt for war, even them the king of Babylon brought captive to Babylon**
> **2 Kings 24:14,16 KJV**

You notice how the king of Babylon carried away all the men and women of value from the land of Israel and left behind the poorest of the land. The craftsmen and blacksmiths were included in that number. What was he looking for? He was looking for people who would add value to his nation and the economy of the nation. It is time for us in the body of Christ to be a blessing to the families of the earth. We are to add so much value to the world around us. This should be known as our trademark as the church of the Lord Jesus Christ. Here, we preach the gospel of results as a means to manifesting His light and love to all humanity. This is a huge part of the corporate assignment of the Great Commission entrusted to the church — transforming the nations for Jesus. The human race is able to see our light so shine that they'll glorify our Father in heaven. From now on, think value and bring value to your world.

THE ATTITUDE PRINCIPLE

CHAPTER 5

THE ATTITUDE PRINCIPLE

Attitude is everything when it comes to our success both in life and in the kingdom. My definition of attitude is responding to any situation the right way leading to a favorable outcome. The right attitude puts the power in your hands. It gives you control over the outcome of any situation. Placing that kind of a power in your hands is quite remarkable because it exempts you from the control of both men and circumstances. No matter what then, you win. You win because you are in charge of the outcome. Anything that's not a part of God's will for your life is changeable and reversible. The right decisions, by necessity, will impose the right corresponding actions resulting in the right corresponding outcomes. Doing right by God and doing right by people will always put you over in life no matter the odds against you. If we do what the Word of God commands us to do in relation to any given circumstance, we will always win. God's Word, therefore, is God's wisdom on all matters of life. In this life, it is not what happens to you that's the issue, but how you choose to respond to what happens is key. I have learned by experience that no matter how bad, dark or unfavorable a situation may be, with faith, patience and the right attitude, you'll emerge triumphant. We will see that Jacob, the covenant man, experienced injustice from his own uncle, Laban, on some many different levels. And, as unfair and inhumane as some of these were, he made a decision to do right by God. And that decision was rewarded with

God's favor.

Laban Breaches the Original Contract with Jacob

"What wages do you want?" Laban asked again. Jacob replied, "Don't give me anything. Just do this one thing, and I'll continue to tend and watch over your flocks. Let me inspect your flocks today and remove all the sheep and goats that are speckled or spotted, along with all the black sheep. Give these to me as my wages. In the future, when you check on the animals you have given me as my wages, you'll see that I have been honest. If you find in my flock any goats without speckles or spots, or any sheep that are not black, you will know that I have stolen them from you."
Genesis 30:31-33 NLT.

Jacob and Laban had agreed on a form of partnership in the business. A tiny fraction of the equity share would go to Jacob. Jacob's shares in the company included owning the speckled and spotted sheep and goats, which were a rare breed and a few in number. Jacob was not going to become rich off of this particular color of sheep and goats. Jacob simply wanted to feel like he owned something to his name, and was willing to build his wealth, one baby step at a time for as long as it'll take. Through an equity share, Jacob was hoping to build something far better than his annual wages. The need for ownership was paramount for him. It afforded him a sense of freedom and ownership which are necessary keys to building wealth. However, that plan didn't work. Laban the trickster had played him again with no regard for the business contract they had agreed upon.

"All right," Laban replied. "It will be as you say"
Genesis 30:34 NLT

Laban hastily agreed to the contract because he knew that the speckled and spotted ones were too few in-between. In his heart, he became so excited about the contract, and strongly felt that Jacob had placed himself in a worse situation. As a result of the contract, Laban believed that Jacob was going to be indebted to him for life. Why Laban wouldn't want Jacob, his own son in-law to prosper is quite baffling. This was the husband to his two daughters and the father to his grandchildren, and all twelve of them. What would Jacob's impoverishment accomplish for him? Wouldn't the prosperity of the entire family benefit them all the more? It was all about control. He simply wanted everyone at his mercy. And this is a part of the reason why you should never be at the mercy of anyone, dead or alive. This is why you're not going to be at the mercy of a job. God wants you to own multiple streams of income, and that way, you'll live in financial freedom.

It's okay to Believe God for Multiple Streams of Income

The Bible gives us some clue as to how many streams of income we should have, and I personally believe this to be the minimum we should all attain to in life. Every day, I hear of some believer losing their job or being laid off their job, and as a consequence, begins a financial downward spiral leading to a complete financial devastation. The time has come upon us as believers never to be at the mercy of a job or employment. We need a new mind shift here. We need to break free from the creditor. We need to live in financial freedom. And, I am more convinced now than ever that this is God's will for the church. We clearly see this sequence in Scripture: "Go, sell the oil, pay your debt, and live you and your sons of the rest — 2 kings 4:7. All financial debts must be paid in full to fully enjoy financial freedom. Debt, like a dead-weight, needs to be laid aside so we can run the race of our lives more effectively. Working a job as the main source of our provision in life has been engrained into our subconscious minds for centuries, even from infant hood; and unfortunately, has formed a huge part of our belief system. Why isn't our financial culture formed on the basis of training all citizens on owning multiple streams of income? Why isn't it an empowerment towards financial freedom? Why didn't anyone teach us how to build financial wealth as a huge part of our academic system? Who even suggested that the credit system has to be the norm for people? Take some time and ponder these vital questions. It is not wise to have all your eggs in one basket. It is never wise to have only one stream of income. In fact, one stream of income can turn out to be a very poor financial decision.

A river flows out of Eden to water the garden and from there divides into four rivers. The first is named Pishon; it flows through Havilah where there is gold. The gold of this land is good. The land is also known for a sweet-scented resin and the onyx stone. The second river is named Gihon; it flows through the land of Cush. The third river is named Hiddekel and flows east of Assyria. The fourth river is the Euphrates   Genesis 2:10 MSG.

Here, we see a river source splitting into four streams. These four rivers watered large portions of lands the size of nations. These four rivers are as follows: Pishon, Gihon, Hiddekel and Euphrates. And these four rivers are mainly financial streams, and their meanings reveal it as such. Pishon means increase; Gihon means bursting forth; Tigris or Hiddekel means rapid, and Euphrates means fruitfulness. These are the waters needed to water your Eden. Four streams born out of one, like a stem with four branches. Most successful pastors I know have multiple streams of income stemming from one primary root. Everyone has a main root or river source designed to split into multiple streams. Not only is this a possibility, it is God's will for us all to flow into financial freedom.

A Blatant Injustice

Although the contract between Laban and Jacob was well understood, signed and sealed, Laban dishonorably breached it the same day. Acting like the pure narcissist that he was, and without regard to either God nor man, he commanded his children to take away all the speckled and spotted goats, both male and female, and all the black sheep that rightfully belonged to Jacob on a three day journey from where Jacob was.

> **But that very day Laban went out and removed the male goats that were streaked and spotted, all the female goats that were speckled and spotted or had white patches, and all the black sheep. He placed them in the care of his own sons, who took them a three-days' journey from where Jacob was. Meanwhile, Jacob**

stayed and cared for the rest of Laban's flock.
Genesis 30:35-36 NLT.

This action by Laban revealed that he had no ounce of goodwill toward Jacob. He clearly didn't want Jacob to prosper. He simply wanted all that wealth for himself. What a flagrant injustice? After desperately asking Jacob to stay, and finally agreeing to some equity share, he blatantly broke the contract. Now that he had taken away all the speckled and spotted goats and black sheep from Jacob, what was Jacob going to do. Jacob had nothing to work with — no speckled and no spotted goats or black sheep. It's like a farmer trying to grow corn without any corn-seed. Jacob had worked so hard to get to this place, and finally hoped for his financial status to turn for the better only to have his own blood relative dash to pieces all his hope for freedom after slaving for fourteen years. What would Jacob do in the light of such an injustice — in the light of such robbery? What should he do? What would you do? The Bible simply told us that Jacob stayed and cared for the rest of Laban's flock. Jacob could have allowed anger, resentment, bitterness distrust, or any number of offenses to take root in his soul, but he didn't. He kept his heart pure and his hands clean. Somehow, he was able to lay all that injustice at the feet of God and chose never to pick it up again. He must have been aware of how much God hates injustice; especially, injustice against the poor and the helpless. He knew that God would avenge for him, and fully trusted God's justice system. And this is what we too must do when a form of injustice has been meted out to us. We must all arrive at a place where we know that all things work together for our good. That we cannot be disadvantaged, not even in the face of the worst injustice.

I believe that Jacob settled the fact that God would come

through for him in a big way, and so should we. It's all about one's attitude. Remember, attitude is the power to respond to any situation in the right way leading to a favorable outcome. Let us learn to take things to God in prayer. In that secret place, let God feel your injustice. Once you lay it at His feet, choose to walk away completely free, and watch God fight for you. The Lord was going to take Jacob on a walk of faith he had never known before. God was going to use this unjust situation in Jacob's life as a lesson for us all in the school of the supernatural. It's a lesson on how to create the life you want, and how to turn anything around in your favor. God was eventually going to hand him the master key to controlling and dominating the world's economy. God was going to show him how to break free from a financial tyrant, and how to never be at the mercy of any employer or any job. If you so desire this freedom, it shall be yours for the taking. Prayerfully proceed.

In this world, a big part of the tribulations we would experience on some level would be maltreatments, mistreatments and all forms of injustices even from those closest to you. And these offenses, if allowed to thrive would create a root of bitterness in your soul. Therefore, learn to guard your heart from being poisoned from the betrayals and disappointments of people. Take every critical judgment with grace. Keep your soul free from pollutants and contaminants. And protect your time and space. One of the things I've been working on is to protect my abiding place more and more each day. Every seed cannot thrive in any soil. Place your soul where it can dance in the sun. Every day, intentionally put yourself in an environment that always brings out the best in you.

E

F P

T O Z

L P E D

P E C F D

E D F C Z P

F E L O P Z D

D E F P O T E C

L F E O D P C T

F D P L T C E O

E F Z O L C F T D

1
2
3
4
5
6
7
8
9
10
11

THE VISION PRINCIPLE

CHAPTER 6

THE VISION PRINCIPLE

Jacob, one day, had to finally narrate to his wives the secret to turning his entire predicament around. After six more years of working for Laban, God had supernaturally taken all the wealth of Laban and transferred it all to Jacob.

But Jacob soon learned that Laban's sons were grumbling about him. "Jacob has robbed our father of everything!" they said. "He has gained all his wealth at our father's expense."
Genesis 31:1 NLT

Here, we see that at the end of it all, Jacob was duly compensated by the God of all justice. It seemed like God did with him what He did with the children of Israel during their four hundred and thirty years of slavery in Egypt. In one night, the night of their emancipation, God transferred the entire wealth of Egypt back to its rightful owners. God must have felt that all of Egypt's glory was built on the back of the slaves, and therefore, rightfully belonged to them. He was simply returning it back in the light of all the injustices that was meted out to them. In the same way, all that wealth that was built by Jacob belonged to him considering the injustices he suffered because it. Jacob would enter the seventh year after the last six years of labor a free man. Yes, like the Israelites, he came out loaded with silver and gold. And I believe, we too, shall enter into our wealthy place loaded with benefits. God wants you free. No man or devil is going to keep you in bondage. No force is going to hold your destiny hostage. Let's all embrace these new paradigms in this season of our lives. God wants so much more for you.

So, what exactly did Jacob tell his wives? How did God change his story?

This story gets more interesting and more exciting here. Jacob carefully narrates this amazing turn-around-story to both Rachel and Leah. He wanted to tell them how God had turned things around for him, and all the amazing lessons he had learned along the way. Pay close attention now and listen with your heart.

> **So, Jacob called Rachel and Leah out to the field where he was watching his flock. He said to them, "I have noticed that your father's attitude toward me has changed. But the God of my father has been with me. You know how hard I have worked for your father, but he has cheated me, changing my wages ten times. But God has not allowed him to do me any harm. For if he said, 'The speckled animals will be your wages,' the whole flock began to produce speckled young. And when he changed his mind and said, 'The striped animals will be your wages,' then the whole flock produced striped young. In this way, God has taken your father's animals and given them to me**
> **Genesis 31:4-9 NLT.**

Jacob again begins by telling his wives about all the injustices he had suffered at the hands of his uncle, Laban. How

Laban had mistreated him changing his wages ten times. Although, Jacob never allowed any form of bitterness to take root in him over all the injustices that were meted out to him by Laban, It was important for Jacob to remember that it was okay to forgive, but not to naively forget, until a track record of trustworthiness was established. Remember this: trust is always earned. God had to come to his defense from Laban's assaults. We notice that no matter how many times Laban tried to change his wages; Jacob came out on top. From previously agreeing to Jacob's ownership of all the speckled and spotted animals, to trying to manipulate his salary at will, and to all the effort he made to sabotage Jacob's success. At whatever turn Laban took, and whatever schemes he used against Jacob, it never worked. In a sense, Jacob became invincible to all of the conniving strategies of Laban. The Bible declares that there's no divination or enchantment against Jacob — Numbers 23:23. God had made him a master chess player in life and business. God had given Jacob the master-key to the economy. He won at every turn. God had given him the secret to controlling market climates and conditions. He even controlled the market laws and market trends just as Solomon owned and controlled all the seaports of his day. God wants us to start playing big in the economies of this world's system. How about controlling the financial systems of this world and doing that all for the glory of God.

For if he said, 'The speckled animals will be your wages,' the whole flock began to produce speckled young. And when he changed his mind and said, 'The striped animals will be your wages,' then the whole flock produced striped young. In this way, God has taken

your father's animals and given them to me
Genesis 31:8-9 NLT.

Jacob had explained to his wives that when Laban wanted the speckled animals as his wages for a specific season, then, all the animals produced speckled. Then, he'll change his mind and say that his wages this time would be spotted; and again, all the flock bore spotted. This is how God transferred all of Laban's wealth to Jacob. But how did Jacob make all the animals produce exactly what he wanted? Better yet, how did he produce speckled and spotted animals to begin with since Laban took away all the existing speckled and spotted animals? These questions bring us to the title of this chapter — vision! Jacob unravels the mystery — a mystery on how God gave him the keys to the kingdom — a lesson of a living faith in God.

The Power of Seeing How God Sees and Naming things How God Names them.

"One time during the mating season, I had a dream and saw that the male goats mating with the females were streaked, speckled, and spotted. Then in my dream, the angel of God said to me, 'Jacob!' And I replied, 'Yes, here I am.' "The angel said, 'Look up, and you will see that only the streaked, speckled, and spotted males are mating with the females of your flock. For I have seen how Laban has treated you   Genesis 31:10-12 NLT.

Jacob told his wives that one time during the mating season, he had had a dream. In the dream, he saw that the male goats that were mating with his female flocks were all streaked, speckled and spotted. This is what he saw. God wanted him to fix his eyes on this picture: "speckled and spotted goats mating with the females of his flock." God wanted that picture transfixed into Jacob's subconscious mind. This dream opened up to Jacob pictures of the supernatural realm; howbeit, it was a real spirit materiality. His work of faith was to see what God was seeing no matter the natural evidence. Faith is the evidence of things spiritually seen — Hebrews 11:1. In the natural, there were no streaked, speckled or spotted animals anywhere because Laban had taken them all away. Yet, Jacob had to stay his eyes on what God was telling him to see. Your vision creates your reality. The visions of your heart are more real than what your optical eyes can see. In God's kingdom, you create realities by vision — by an absorbing gazing vision that becomes one with your spirit and sinks deep down into your subconscious mind.

And in that dream, the angel of God told him to enter into a realm of transfixing his eyes on a superior reality — the faith reality, which is seeing only what God sees and only calling what God calls with no regard for natural evidence. You mean that God gave me the power to create the future I want, the health I want and the life I want? Absolutely yes! This is the law of transformation — the law of transforming anything you want to see into what you want it to be. It is the law of reversing things that you don't like into things that you do like. It is the law of creation and recreation. And what did the angel of God tell him precisely? The angel of God told him to see that only the speckled and spotted animals were mating with the female of his flock. Jacob was not to see anything else but the picture of speckled and spotted animals mating. He cannot look upon anything contrary. He cannot open his mind or thoughts to any other proof or evidence. This was what God wanted him to see, and only this. He could not deviate from it either to the left or to the right. I can imagine Jacob working his farms every day and only seeing these animals in the natural without specks or spots. Now, he had to wear a faith lens. See the natural through supernatural lenses. See health imposed upon the sickness; the wealth imposed upon the poverty; the light overshadowing the darkness, and see it until corruptibility is swallowed by incorruptibility, and mortality by immortality. This vision principle is a most powerful weapon. It is God's way of taking you from point A to point B. This means that any circumstance, no matter how bad is changeable. And you change it by looking at something different. You change it through vision. Your mind must first arrive at where your body would want to go. See that picture and hold that picture until it is sown as a seed in the soil of your subconscious mind.

> **And the Lord said unto Abram, after that Lot was separated from him, Lift up now thine eyes, and look from the place where thou art northward, and southward, and eastward, and westward: For all the land which thou seest, to thee will I give it, and to thy seed forever. Arise, walk through the land in the length of it and in the breadth of it; for I will give it unto thee**
> **Genesis 13:14, 15, 17 KJV**

God revealed this principle of envisioning to Abraham. He told him to look from the place where he was currently to the place where he needed to be. He told Abraham if he could see the land, it will be given to him and his descendants. God gives you what you see, and so does life. Then

God told Abraham to walk in the length and the breath of the land. And he was to walk it in his mind. He was to fully live in the land in his mind and become familiar with it in his mind. He was to arrive before he arrived. This is what vision does. Hello people, we walk by faith, and not by sight!! That is, we function on earth through a different lens. We do not live by natural sight, but by spiritual sight. Let the supernatural drive your actions. Instead of living in the natural, learn to live in the supernatural. Everything and anything in the natural are subject to change at any moment. Focus your sight on the right photographs. Set your eyes on things above. Fix them on the exact outcome you want to see. He who looks shall live — Numbers 21:9. Look at the one who took all the poison of the serpent on His cross to the very last drop. Look and be free.

THE BETHEL PRINCIPLE

Chapter 7

The Bethel Principle

"The angel said, 'Look up, and you will see that only the streaked, speckled, and spotted males are mating with the females of your flock. For I have seen how Laban has treated you. I am the God who appeared to you at Bethel, the place where you anointed the pillar of stone and made your vow to me. Now get ready and leave this country and return to the land of your birth.'"
Genesis 31:12-13 NLT

Right after the angel of God had told him what to do in the dream, the same angel introduced himself to Jacob as the God who had appeared to him at Bethel, the place where Jacob had anointed a stone, and had made his vow to God. So, what happened at Bethel? Jacob had rested his head on a stone pillow to sleep from his weary journey. As he slept, he had a dream. In this dream, he saw a ladder set on earth and reaching into the heavens with the Lord Himself at the very top of the ladder, and the angels descending and ascending on it. These angels of God were simply transporting packages from heaven to earth. Like Jacob, they'll show you how to come out on top every time. They'll show you how to win in this life. Wherever the presence of the Holy Spirit is honored and manifested, there is also mighty manifestations of angelic presences. And these angels are present to minister the program of the Holy Spirit in a meeting. They are carriers of divine gifts from heaven to earth, and they participate fully in the administration of the gifts.

> At sundown he arrived at a good place to set up camp and stopped there for the night. Jacob found a stone to rest his head against and lay down to sleep. As he slept, he dreamed of a stairway that reached from the earth up to heaven. And he saw the angels of God going up and down the stairway. At the top of the stairway stood the Lord, and he said, "I am the Lord, the God of your grandfather Abraham, and the God of your father, Isaac. The ground you are lying on belongs to you. I am giving it to you and your descendants. Your descendants will be as numerous as the dust of the earth! They will spread out in all directions—to the west and the east, to the north and the south. And all the families of the earth will be blessed through you and your descendants. What's more, I am with you, and I will protect you wherever you go. One day I will bring you back to this land. I will not leave you until I have finished giving you everything I have promised you." **Genesis 28:11-15 NLT**

This place that Jacob had had this wonderful spiritual encounter was called Bethel, which means the house of God. It's also called the gate of heaven. He had been shown a ladder connecting two worlds and two realms and two realities. He had been shown that divine transactions can take place between these two realms, and that there's a business partnership between the two. He had been equally shown that the angels of God officiated as the agents over these transactions at both ends. We saw this exemplified in Jacob's life when an angel of God spoke to him in a dream. A dream or vision opens up a portal from the earth into the realm of the heavens, and vice-visa, allowing angels as officiating agents to fully carry out that transaction. The gifts they come bearing are instructions communicated through pictures and words. It was an angel that appeared to Cornelius in a vision as in a dream to Jacob. These instructions through dreams and visions are imported into this realm through obedience. God is still the God of Bethel today, and longs to pour out real solutions to problems plaguing the human race. He wants to pour out abundance of ideas, inventions and innovations that would revolutionize the nations of the earth.

> **Then Jacob awoke from his sleep and said, "Surely the Lord is in this place, and I wasn't even aware of it!" But he was also afraid and said, "What an awesome place this is! It is none other than the house of God, the very gateway to heaven!" The next morning Jacob got up very early. He took the stone he had rested his head against, and he set it upright as a memorial pillar. Then he poured olive oil over it. He named that place Bethel (which means "house of God"), although it was previously called Luz.   Genesis 28:16-19 NLT**

Jacob called Bethel, "the very gateway to heaven." But it is also God's gateway to earth. As we give ourselves to the things of the Spirit, dreams and visions would become common place occurrences. Joel 2:28 speaks of our sons and daughters having visions as a major manifestation of the Spirit in the last days. As we give ourselves to a deeper communion with God, praying effectively with our spirits in the Spirit, we shall have the eyes of our hearts more illuminated. Before prophets were called prophets, they were called seers because people of the Spirit see quite often. People given over to prayer are called watchers because of their ability to see a bunch of things in the spirit. In the book of Ezekiel, we see dramatic manifestations of the Spirit in all forms of visions, trances and dreams. In the book of Acts, where the activities of God's Spirit were so evident, we see the abundance of dreams and visions.

Bethel is heaven's open portal to earth, and earth's open portal to heaven. And it all happens at the place of an encounter with God. May we graduate from praying mere prayers to praying prayers that connect us to experiencing God on a daily basis. God's house, Bethel, ultimately is a place of transfiguration — an irreversible impact of the Spirit on the human soul. Every dynamic change in a person's heart come from a true encounter with God's Spirit. In this place, and at this spot, you'll see things and hear things that'll deeply impact your life forever. Learn to practice the presence of God. It is actually simple. Learn to acknowledge God in all your ways, and He shall direct your paths. Thank Him all the time for everything at every single opportunity you get. Thank Him for waking you up; thank Him on your way to work; thank Him when you arrive at work; thank Him again as you get ready to work; thank Him during your breaks; thank Him again for making your day a success, for leading you to a soul to win over for Christ, and for all the victories for the day; thank Him for bringing you back home safely; thank Him for all the wonderful things that would happen before bedtime etc. You'll always be so filled with God's Spirit when you acknowledge Him all the time. Keeping yourself filled with God's Spirit is how you live under His leadership. Living under His leadership is how you're constantly led by His voice; and obeying his voice is how you win, always. It is that simple.

THE CONVERSION PRINCIPLE

CHAPTER 8

THE CONVERSION PRINCIPLE

The conversion principle is the art of converting spiritual realities into physical realities. A dream remains in a dream form, until it is converted. Ideas remain ideas, until they're converted. Jacob had to find a way to apply what was revealed to him in a spirit-substance form into something tangible and useable. God had given him the blueprint to wealth creation in a dream, but he had to find a way to make it work for him in a pragmatic way. Jacob had been shown how to create something out of nothing, and how to recreate any situation into a favorable outcome by faith. And through the eyes of faith, he could only see a speckled and spotted flock of animals. What he saw in the physical and natural realms made no difference; no, not even for a moment. However, the vision of the speckled and spotted animals had become a settled fact in his heart because it had grown to dominate his spirit. But how was Jacob going to convert what he had seen in a spirit-substance form into a physical form where he could both apply it and use it. I believe the answer to that question didn't come overnight. He had to probably hold that vision in thought form for days, and possibly weeks. He had to rub minds with God — Isaiah 1:18. He had to constantly ask the question, "how do I convert this vision into a useable form?" Right questions invoke the right answers. He'd had to have a mental conversation with God.

Meanwhile, as Peter was puzzling over the vision, the Holy Spirit said to him Acts 10:19 NLT.

You're going have to do what Peter did. You're going to have to puzzle over your faith photographs or faith snapshots for a while, until God's voice is heard, and His instructions followed. God's Spirit speaks, guides and instructs while you're musing over your visions. Again, what exactly did Jacob see? He saw only the speckled and spotted animals. Now that he had cultivated his faith for speckled and spotted animals, and was totally convinced that God was going to create them from the other flock that wasn't speckled, spotted or streaked, he had to find a practical way to get the animals to simply see what he was seeing. But how exactly was he going to accomplish that? How was he going to convert this spirit reality into physical materiality? How was he going get the animals that were not speckled, spotted or streaked to become speckled, spotted and streaked? His first business was to keep seeing what God had told him to see, and to keep saying what God had told him to say. According to the Bible, God will give you what you see–(Genesis 13:14-17, Genesis 15:2); and He will also give you what you say — (Mark 11:23; Numbers 14:28). In other words, these three things need to come into perfect alignment with each other, and remain consistent, until the Spirit of the Lord broods over the issues in your mind. And these three things are: "thinking the same thoughts, saying the same words, and displaying the same actions," until the idea on how to actually convert spirit materiality into physical materiality happens. This is how we come into agreement with God. It happens when we have the same mind with God. In the process of rubbing minds together, we exchange our questions with

His answers. With the heart, man believes unto righteousness, and with the mouth, confession is made unto salvation — Romans 10:10. With the organ of our spirit-man, we believe or see things eye to eye with God. Can two walk together except they agree (Amos 3:3)? The Holy Spirit of God gets to work once we come into alignment with God's truth. God told Jacob in the dream to only fix his eyes on seeing the speckled, spotted and streaked animals mating with the females of his flock.

He must keep that picture before his eyes engraved into his subconscious mind. It must become his predominant thought permeating his whole being; including his emotions, decisions, words and actions. And as he continues to ask for the practical knowledge on how to convert his faith photographs into physical reality, the Holy Spirit will commence the work of showing him how to do it each step of the way. In his meditations, contemplations and musings over his vision of the speckled and spotted animals, he had come to know the following things:

1. The speckled and spotted animals were going to be created from the non-speckled and spotted ones
2. It would happen during their mating season
3. The mating process must take place at the watering troughs. Jacob had to find a way to present the same faith photographs to the non-speckled and spotted animals, so that, they too, will see what he had seen, and produce after the speckled and spotted faith photographs before them as they mated.
4. In order for the animals to produce offspring that were speckled and spotted, he had to create a speckled and spotted fence, which was going to be placed before them while they mated. The Holy

Spirit was going to have to show him how to do it perfectly to produce the desired result.

Then Jacob took some fresh branches from poplar, almond, and plane trees and peeled off strips of bark, making white streaks on them. Then he placed these peeled branches in the watering troughs where the flocks came to drink, for that was where they mated. And when they mated in front of the white-streaked branches, they gave birth to young that were streaked, speckled, and spotted. Jacob separated those lambs from Laban's flock. And at mating time he turned the flock to face Laban's animals that were streaked or black. This is how he built his own flock instead of increasing Laban's. Whenever the stronger females were ready to mate, Jacob would place the peeled branches in the watering troughs in front of them. Then they would mate in front of the branches. But he didn't do this with the weaker ones, so the weaker lambs belonged to Laban, and the stronger ones were Jacob's. As a result, Jacob became very wealthy, with large flocks of sheep and goats, female and male servants, and many camels and donkeys
Genesis 30:37-43 NLT.

Did you see how that conversion happened? Jacob created a mobile fence that was speckled, spotted and streaked, and placed it before the watering troughs were the animals came to mate. Those non-speckled, non-spotted and non-streaked animals gave birth according to the vision of what Jacob had seen and settled in his heart, and according to the picture and colors on the mobile fence. They produced after what they saw. God's Spirit simply re-engineered their DNA as they looked at the speckled and spotted fence and produced their young after the colors that were on the fence. This is exactly the same way God transforms us from glory to glory.

But we all, with unveiled face, beholding as in a mirror the glory of the Lord, are being transformed into the same image from glory to glory, just as by the Spirit of the Lord.
2 Corinthians 3:18 NKJV

If this type of transformation can happen for animals, based on simply looking at the colors on a mobile fence, how much more for those of us who are made in the image of God, and are beholding the word of God? How much more I say? According to God's word, we become what we behold. What have you been looking at lately? What do you have your mind fixed on? You'll produce after what you see. Instead of looking at that disease, look at your healing. Instead of lack and want and poverty, look at the prosperity and abundance all around you. Instead of looking at all the depressive things; lift up your eyes and see happiness. This is how it works. What you continue to look at magnifies and amplifies. The more of the problem you see, the less of the solution you'll see. Abraham, the father of our faith, too, had to stop looking at his hundred-year-old impotent body, and at Sarah's ninety-year-old barren womb, if he was ever going to produce an Isaac. And, although, that was his physical reality, it wasn't his spiritual reality. He simply had to switch lenses and started seeing things from God's vantage position. It's not the sickness in your body sister that's the problem here, it's the lens you're wearing. Somebody needs a Holy Ghost cloth so that they can wipe off the fog on their eyeglasses and look through it again with the eyes of faith.

Tongues and Interpretation

Oh, that my people will look again, and live. Take off the scale of doubt and fear from your eyes, and put on the lens of faith, and see all the possibilities lying before you. See, and live saith the Holy Ghost. Look, and live. Look into my word and absorb what my Spirit is showing to you in this season. Yea, and truthfully, my word cannot fail to produce. Your answer is in my word. Let my Spirit teach you its profound truths. It's in my word. And as you embrace Him, love and cherish Him, and behold him day and night; yea, as you kiss my word, and become one with Him, you shall walk into possibilities you never thought possible saith the Spirit of the Lord.

We see that no matter how many times Laban changed Jacob's wages; He came out on top because God had given him the master-key on how to create what he wanted at will.

For if he said, 'The speckled animals will be your wages,' the whole flock began to produce speckled young. And when he changed his mind and said, 'The striped animals will be your wages,' then the whole flock produced striped young. In this way, God has taken your father's animals and given them to me
Genesis 31:8-9 NLT.

Jacob wasn't at the mercy of a man or a job. He had in his possession the exact knowledge on how to create the life he wanted, and the knowledge to create it at will. He commanded the very science of wealth creation at his fingertips. And his knowledge of wealth creation wasn't dependent on changing climates, seasons or conditions. His key to wealth creation was a perfect science given to him by God. God wants us all to become masters at building wealth. He literally wants us to have control of the market laws and market trends. He wants us to control the chain of supply and demand. God wants us to play big in the economies of this world. God wants us to put a money-making machine in place that keeps on producing at will, until all the earth is impacted by the gospel of the Lord Jesus Christ. A huge part of the coming glory of the church is a complete takeover of the financial institutions of this world's system — Haggai 2:8-9. It is the creation of a new bank and banking system that has never existed before. The bank of the Most High God fully at work in the earth, and at the disposal of the hands of the sons of God. The order of the Abrahamic wealth — a prototype we see in Isaac is that of one man becoming richer than a nation — Genesis 26:12-14. The time for us to lend to nations has come. Think big; dream big, and watch God make whatever you can believe Him for happen for you.

CPSIA information can be obtained
at www.ICGtesting.com
Printed in the USA
JSHW042358300420
5387JS00004B/12